The Real Alcázar

...ville

The Jardín del Chorrón ("Garden of the Stream")

REALES ALCAZARES

From the Muslim Al Qasr to the Castilian Alcazar

SITUATED NEAR THE CATHEDRAL AND THE GENERAL ARCHIVE OF THE INDIES IN ONE OF SEVILLE'S MOST EMBLEMATIC AREAS, THE REAL ALCÁZAR RISES UPRIGHT, STRONG, VIGOROUS AND EXPECTANT IN THE FACE OF HISTORY.

THE TERM "ALCÁZAR" COMES FROM THE HISPANO-ARABIC WORD "ALQÁȘR" MEANING "ROYAL HOUSE" OR "ROOM OF THE PRINCE" (WHETHER FORTIFIED OR NOT).

THE ORIGINAL BUILDING WAS TRADITIONALLY BELIEVED TO BE THE PALACE KNOWN AS THE AL-QASR DAR AL IMARA ("HOUSE OF THE GOVERNMENT") BUILT BY ADB AL-RAHMAN III IN THE 10TH CENTURY. EXCAVATIONS IN RECENT YEARS, HOWEVER, HAVE REVEALED THAT THE ENCLOSURE ACTUALLY DATES FROM AROUND THE END OF THE 11TH CENTURY.

OVER THE AGES, THIS ROYAL BUILDING HAS BEEN THE HOME OF MANY MONARCHS, MAJOR HISTORICAL EVENTS AFFECTING THE WHOLE WORLD HAVE TAKEN PLACE WITHIN ITS WALLS, AND IT CONTINUES TO BE ONE OF THE MOST IMPORTANT BUILDINGS IN ALL OF SPAIN. IT CAN ALSO BE REGARDED AS THE OLDEST SPANISH ROYAL PALACE STILL IN USE, AS EVEN TODAY IT IS ONE OF THE OFFICIAL RESIDENCES OF THE KING OF SPAIN.

The royal coat of arms on tiling over the arch between the Plaza del Triunfo ("Square of Triumph") and the Patio de Banderas ("Court of Flags").

pp. 6-7

View of the Giralda by night from the Real Alcázar: "On one occasion she bade me go and challenge the famous giantess of Seville, La Giralda by name, who is as mighty and strong as if made of brass, and though never stirring from one spot, is the most restless and changeable woman in the world." (Second Volume of *The Ingenious Gentleman Don Quixote of La Mancha*, Miguel de Cervantes).

p. 8

View of the Alcázar wall from the Callejón del Agua ("Water Alley"), so called because the wall was used by the Muslims in the transportation of the water which supplied the palace. This section, which adjoined the old Jewish Quarter, belongs to the 11th-century Muslim palace.

p. 9

View of the wall from the Callejón de la Judería ("Jewry Alley"). Part of the palace wall encircles the old Jewish quarter. With its narrow streets, white houses and flowery courtyards and balconies, the Santa Cruz district is even today a typical example of the mediaeval Andalusian neighbourhood.

p. 10

The main entrance to the Alcázar, the Puerta del León ("Lion Gate"), takes its name from the 19th-century tilework inlaid above it (José Gestoso y Pérez, 1894). A crowned lion rampant reminds us that the area we are about to enter is a royal site. The lion holds a cross in its claws and bears a banner with Gothic script reading "Ad Utrumque" —"Prepared for all".

p. 11

With the Puerta del León and part of its walls rising over the Plaza del Triunfo, the Cathedral and General Archive of the Indies form an extraordinary backdrop.

From the Muslim Al Qasr to the Castilian Alcazar

pp. 12-13

A flag with the inscription NO&DO (the Seville Council motto and logotype) flies over the Alcázar. It is replaced by the royal banner when the King is in residence at the palace.

NO&DO is a hieroglyph referring to the city's loyalty to Alfonso X "the Wise" during the war between the king and his son Don Sancho in the 13th century. Alfonso won the final battle and in gratitude to Seville designed this motto, consisting of the syllables NO and DO with an 8 representing a skein of wool ("madeja" in Spanish) between. When read aloud it forms the words "NO MADEJA DO", which can be translated as a reference to the fact that the people of Seville "did not abandon me" in the face of Don Sancho's attack.

p. 14

From the former residents of the Alcázar the kings of Castile inherited the belief that water was the source of life on earth and the essence from which Allah had created man. Islam ascribed it with the most sacred of attributes, as a giver of life and a source of sustenance and purification.

p. 15

View of the Patio del Yeso ("Court of Stuccowork"), from the Sala de Justicia ("Hall of Justice") or Sala del Consejo del Rey Don Pedro I ("Council Room of King Peter I"). This first example of Mudéjar architecture was built by Alfonso XI in the mid-14th century following his victory at the Battle of Río Salado. In this room, Peter I is said to have ordered the murder of his stepbrother *Don* Fadrique in this room.

p. 16-17

Remains of the 12th-century Almohad Palace in the Patio del Yeso. This side section of wall is formed with multifoil arches displaying *sebka* or diamond-pattern panels —decoration typical of the period. The influence of the Almohad dynasty on Seville, then capital of this Muslim kingdom, was extremely important. The Almohads were ruling the city when it was conquered by Saint Ferdinand III in 1248.

Seville, the Centre of the Indies Monopoly: The House of Trade

THE HOUSE OF TRADE WITH THE INDIES WAS ESTABLISHED IN 1503 IN SEVILLE TO ORGANISE AND RE-GULARISE TRADE AND NAVIGATION BETWEEN SPAIN AND THE NEW WORLD. FOR THE FIRST YEAR OF ITS EXISTENCE IT WAS BASED IN SEVILLE'S ATARANZAS OR SHIPYARDS BUT WAS SOON TRANSFERRED TO THE REAL ALCÁZAR, WHERE IT REMAINED UNTIL ITS OFFICIAL RE-ESTABLISHMENT IN CADIZ IN 1717. DUE TO ITS STRATEGIC POSITION, SEVILLE WAS THE IDEAL CITY GEOGRAPHICALLY TO SERVE THE PURPOSES OF THE HOUSE OF TRADE AND, AS AN INLAND PORT A HUNDRED KILOMETRES FROM THE COAST, WAS WELL PROTECTED FROM ATTACK. FURTHERMORE, IT HAD BEEN A COMMERCIAL PORT SINCE ANCIENT TIMES AND WITH THE DISCOVERY OF AMERICA BECAME OF WORLDWIDE IMPORTANCE.

THIS RIVER PORT HELD THE MONOPOLY ON THE TRADE ROUTE TO THE INDIES, CONTROLLING ALL INCOMING AND OUTGOING GOODS. THE HOUSE OF TRADE BECAME A CENTRE FOR COSMOGRAPHIC, CARTOGRAPHIC AND NAUTICAL STUDIES WHICH WERE ASSIGNED TO THE PILOT MAJORS WHO RAN THE INSTITUTION.

IT WAS THERE WHERE THE FIRST GEOGRAPHICAL MAP OF THE NEW WORLD WAS DRAWN AND MAGELLAN'S FIRST CIRCUMNAVIGATION OF THE WORLD WAS PLANNED. MAJOR HISTORICAL FIGURES LIKE AMERIGO VESPUCCI, WHO BECAME A PILOT MAJOR IN 1508, PLAYED AN EXTREMELY IMPORTANT PART IN THE DEVELOPMENT OF THE HOUSE OF TRADE.

Detail of the canvas *Our Lady of Navigators* on the altarpiece in the Sala de Audiencias ("Audience Room") in the House of Trade.

pp. 20-21

Through the three arches in the wall and on the other side of the Patio del León stands the Patio de la Montería ("Court of the Hunt"), the atrium of the Mudéjar Palace and the House of Trade. The courtyard takes its name from the royal beaters who gathered there before hunts.

p. 22

The House of Trade was established to promote and regulate Indies trade and travel between Spain and the New World. The altarpiece in the Sala de Audiencias was painted by Alejo Fernández in the 16th century.

p. 23

The main façade of the Palacio de Don Pedro I ("Palace of Peter I"), viewed from the House of Trade's Renaissance gallery.

p. 24

The Cuarto del Almirante ("Admiral's Hall") was one of the rooms in which the cosmographic and nautical ventures in the New World were planned. It takes its name from the Tribunal del Almirantazgo de Castilla ("Tribunal of the Admiralty of Castile"), a title created by the first kings of Castile after the reconquest of Seville.

p. 25

The Our Lady of Navigators altar in the Sala de Audiencias. The image in the centre is that of the Virgin Mary sheltering figures from the Old and New Worlds under her open mantle. She was also known as "Our Lady of Fair Winds" as sailors bound for the Indies traditionally prayed to her for "fair winds" on their voyages before setting sail.

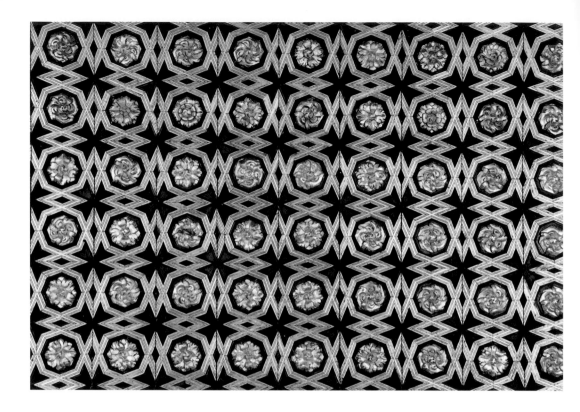

p. 26

Detail of the coffered ceiling of geometric forms and gilt fleurons in the Sala de Audiencias. Dating from the 16th century, the ceiling was a fusion of the original Muslim structure with the innovative decorative motifs of the Renaissance.

p. 27

Columbus's coat of arms consists of elements of intense symbolic power: the castle and lion, representing the kingdoms of Isabella I above, with the islands discovered by the Admiral and anchors alluding to seafaring below. The coat of arms is framed by two, larger anchors and a band with the inscription: "A Castilla y a León nuevo mundo dio Colón" ("For Castile and Leon a new world Columbus won.")

The Residence of Kings:
The Cuarto Real Alto

THE FIRST FLOOR OF THE BUILDING DATES FROM THE PERIOD OF PETER I, KNOWN AS BOTH "THE CRUEL" AND "THE JUST", WHO ORDERED TWO ROOMS BUILT THERE FOR WINTER USE. OVER THE CENTURIES, SUCCESSIVE OCCUPANTS OF THE CUARTO REAL ALTO ("UPPER ROYAL APARTMENTS") ADDED NEW ROOMS AND ADAPTED THE EXISTING ONES TO THE NEEDS OF THEIR TIME.

FOR THE PERIODS WHEN THE CATHOLIC MONARCHS WOULD BE IN RESIDENCE IN SEVILLE, IT WAS NECESSARY TO ADAPT THE UPPER PALACE FOR THEIR PRIVATE USE, HENCE MORE ROOMS WERE ADDED. YEARS LATER, THE EMPEROR CHARLES I ORDERED ALTERATIONS MADE TO THIS AREA IN PREPARATION FOR HIS MARRIAGE TO HIS COUSIN PRINCESS ISABELLA OF PORTUGAL IN 1526; THESE INCLUDED IMPROVEMENTS TO THE MEDIAEVAL ROOMS AND NEW CONSTRUCTIONS LIKE THE GALERÍA ALTA ("UPPER GALLERY") IN THE PATIO DE LAS DONCELLAS ("COURTYARD OF THE DAMSELS").

THE ALCÁZAR EXPERIENCED ITS TIME OF GREATEST SPLENDOUR UNDER PHILIP II. BY THEN SEVILLE HAD BECOME A COSMOPOLITAN CITY, THE NERVE CENTRE OF THE INDIES PROJECT AND ONE OF THE MOST DENSELY-POPULATED CITIES IN EUROPE.

ALTHOUGH FURTHER RENOVATIONS ON A MORE LIMITED SCALE WERE SUBSEQUENTLY MADE BY PHILIP IV AND PHILIP V, IN THE 19TH CENTURY ISABELLA II ORDERED A FAR-REACHING SERIES OF ALTERATIONS.

TODAY, THE CUARTO REAL ALTO CONTINUES TO REFLECT THE MAJESTY OF BYGONE AGES AND IS STILL USED AS THE OFFICIAL RESIDENCE OF THE KING AND QUEEN OF SPAIN WHEN THEY ARE IN SEVILLE FOR OFFICIAL OCCASIONS.

Detail of the Oratorio de Isabel La Católica ("Oratory of Isabella The Catholic"), decorated with smooth coloured tiles designed by Niculoso Pisano (1504).

p. 30

The Oratorio de Isabel La Católica, decorated with Renaissance-style Sevillian tiling. At the centre, the Virgin Mary visits her cousin St Elizabeth in a charming tribute to the Catholic Queen (whose name can also be translated as Elizabeth). The whole is surrounded by the symbolism of the Tree of Jesse, who is depicted in a reclining position, sprouting the branches of the Virgin Mary's genealogical tree.

pp. 30-31

Detail of the *Annunciation of the Virgin Mary*. The Virgin is surrounded by Renaissance elements and typically Castilian motifs such as pomegranates in an allusion to the conquest of the Muslim kingdom by the Catholic Monarchs, whose initials appear among the ornamentation. A complete novelty in Sevillian decoration, the technique of painting on a smooth ceramic surface and the inclusion of Renaissance motifs was introduced by Niculoso Pisano.

pp. 32-33

The Galería Alta ("Upper Gallery") in the Patio de las Muñecas ("Court of the Dolls"). The decoration of the Mudéjar panels on the original 14th-century ground floor was reproduced on the mezzanine and first floors, added in the reign of Isabella II.

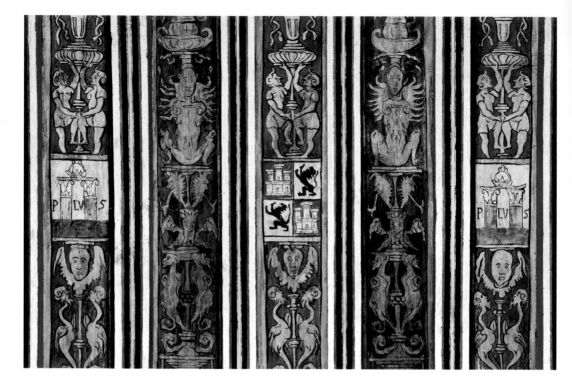

p. 34

Details of the decoration on the coffered ceilings in the Mirador de los Reyes Católicos ("*Mirador* of the Catholic Monarchs"). During restoration work on the ceilings, a prayer to the Virgin Mary was uncovered beneath various layers of paint. It is thought that this ceiling may originally have come from the Sala del Techo de Carlos V ("Charles V Ceiling Room") on the ground floor, which in turn could have been the Chapel in the Mudéjar Palace.

p. 35

The panels forming the coffers in the Sala del Mirador de los Reyes Católicos ("*Mirador* of the Catholic Monarchs Room") display Renaissance decoration and the lion and castle alternating with the shield with the Emperor Charles V's "Plus Ultra" ("Beyond") emblem, representing the dynamism and expansion of Charles's empire as symbolised by the legendary pillars of Hercules.

pp. 36-37

Details of the decoration on the coffered ceilings in the Dormitorio de Don Pedro I ("Bedroom of King Peter I"). The compositions on Mudéjar coffered ceilings tend to be based on ribbons forming stars. Many of these pieces were later gilded, particularly in the 16th century.

p. 38

The Mudéjar perfection of the Dormitorio de Don Pedro I is evident in the combination of the plaster decoration of plant motifs and Arabic inscriptions and the ceramics of the tiling on the wall.

p. 39

Bas-relief of Charles V in the Galería Alta of the Patio de las Doncellas. Following the Emperor Charles V's marriage, there began one of the most important phases of renovation in the history of the palace and a period which saw the introduction of Renaissance elements.

pp. 40-42

This corridor consists of a series of semi-circular arches resting on marble columns. In the decoration, Renaissance motifs alternate with portraits of a lady and gentleman (traditionally associated with the Emperor and Empress) together with emblems from the imperial heraldry.

p. 43

The Sala de Audiencias is one of the two oldest rooms in the Cuarto Alto Real. It was built in the 14th century to form part of Peter I's winter chambers. The typically Mudéjar walls are adorned with traditional Arabic plant motifs, *sebka* panels and epigraphic cartouches combined with the heraldic emblems of Peter of Castile, Leon and the Order of the Band.

p. 44

Detail of the ribbon-design coffered ceiling. After numerous restorations, it was almost entirely rebuilt in the early-19th century.

p. 45

Of special interest in the Sala de Audiencias are the two columns with caliphal capitals carved by Muslim craftsmen. The decoration of the capitals evokes the honeycomb, originally associated with oriental art. In accordance with the tastes of the age, this kind of capital was often gilded.

The Splendour of Mudéjar Civil Architecture: The Palacio de Don Pedro I

THIS PALACE WAS BUILT (1364-1366) BY ORDER OF PETER I OF CASTILE. ITS TOTALLY UNIQUE STYLE IS THE MOST OUTSTANDING EXAMPLE OF MUDÉJAR ART FOUND ANYWHERE ON THE IBERIAN PENINSULA AND FIRST APPEARED DURING THE RECONQUEST, IN SOME AREAS CO-EXISTING WITH OTHER EUROPEAN STYLES SUCH AS GOTHIC AND RENAISSANCE.

MUDÉJAR WAS THE ARTISTIC EXPRESSION OF A SOCIETY IN WHICH CHRISTIANS, MUSLIMS AND JEWS LIVED ALONGSIDE EACH OTHER. THE NAME COMES FROM THE HISPANO-ARABIC WORD *MUDAJJAN*, MEANING "DOMESTICATED" OR "SUBDUED", IN A REFERENCE TO MUSLIMS WHO PAID A SPECIAL TAX ALLOWING THEM TO LIVE AMONG CHRISTIANS WITHOUT HAVING TO RENOUNCE THEIR RELIGION. AS IT PROVED SO DIFFICULT FOR THE CHRISTIANS TO REFILL THE CITIES, MUSLIMS WERE ALLOWED TO REMAIN IN THE RECONQUERED TERRITORIES. THIS SOCIAL SITUATION FACILITATED THE APPEARANCE OF A NEW ARTISTIC STYLE IN WHICH TWO TRADITIONS —CHRISTIAN AND ISLAMIC— MERGED.

THE CONSTRUCTION OF THE MUDÉJAR PALACE MARKS THE PEAK OF THE PROCESS OF REINTEGRATION AND CULTURAL EXCHANGE IN SOUTHERN EUROPE, DESPITE PERIODS OF WAR WITH THE NASRID KINGDOM. PETER I BROUGHT THE BEST MASTER BUILDERS FROM GRANADA AND TOLEDO TO WORK ON HIS PALACE IN COLLABORATION WITH THE LOCAL MUDÉJAR CRAFTSMEN.

WITH ITS COMPOSITIONS AND THE MATERIALS —BRICK, CERAMICS, WOOD AND PLASTER— USED IN ITS MAKING, THE MUDÉJAR PALACE WAS HEIR TO THE HISPANO-MUSLIM TRADITION. MARBLE WAS USED ONLY IN SUPPORTS, COLUMNS AND CAPITALS.

Detail of the coloured stucco wall decoration in the Sala del Príncipe ("Room of the Prince") in the Mudéjar Palace.

p. 48

The Palace of Peter I. On the other side of the three wall arches, the magnificent Mudéjar Palace main gate leads into the Patio de la Montería. Laid out like an altarpiece, this portal is a synthesis of the inside of the building.

p. 49

The central section of the Mudéjar Palace façade contains various geminated windows with exquisite columns and capitals. The arch edges are adorned with ceramics.

pp. 50-51

Detail of the decoration on the main façade. The Mudéjar style is eclectic in that it contains features from the two cultures: multifoil arches, *sebka* diamond-pattern and plant motif decoration (*ataurique*) in the Muslim tradition, together with the coats of arms of Castile, Leon and the Order of the Band (created by Alfonso XI after his victory at the Battle of Río Salado and inherited by his son Peter I of Castile). The three shields appear throughout the building. Alternating with these decorative elements are inscriptions in praise of God such as "The Empire of Allah", "Thanks be to Allah" and also of the king: "In greatness and ostentation this house is unique."

pp. 52-53

An inscription in Gothic characters on the upper section of the Mudéjar Palace façade translates as: "The most high and most noble and most powerful and most victorious Peter, King of Castile and of Leon by the grace of God, ordered this fortress and these palaces and these façades built, which was done in the year one thousand four hundred and two." The date in the inscription corresponds to the Julian calendar, which came into force in 38 B.C. In the manner of an orle, another Arabic inscription with white and blue tiles that is Kufic in style reads: "And there is no victor but Allah" and is repeated several times. The roof above the façade is of wood adorned with stalactite-work.

pp. 54-55

The Patio de las Doncellas. The central courtyard has recently recovered its original layout. Though for almost 500 years it was paved with marble and contained a Renaissance fountain, it is now exactly as it was in the 14th century. It was designed with a typically Nasrid central pool and the trees at its sides stand at a lower level so that their tops will conceal the central courtyard in imitation of a leafy forest ideal for roaming: indeed, the area was intended as a re-creation of paradise.

RDOR DON PEDRO POR LA GRACIA DE DIOS REY DE CASTIELLA ET DE LEON MA

ADAS QUE FUE FECHO EN LA ERA DE MILL ET QUATROCIENTOS Y DOS

pp. 56-57

Wall decoration in the Patio de las Doncellas. The use of stucco to face buildings was a Mudéjar adaptation of a Muslim tradition. The geometric ribbon motifs, the schematic plant decoration and the cartouches with Kufic inscriptions are repeated again and again over the entire wall.

p. 58

Detail of an arch in the Patio de las Doncellas. In the Middle Ages, a century after the reconquest of the city, Pedro I looked to local Muslim architecture when he built his Mudéjar Palace. Hence the profusion of multifoil arches and plaster diamond clusters.

p. 59

The Patio de las Doncellas lay at the centre of the public area in the Palacio de Don Pedro I. Much emphasis was placed on water, for, in addition to its aesthetic function —being pleasant to the ear and reflecting light— it also refreshes the atmosphere. In a stunning optical effect, the still water in the pool reflects the façade with its stuccowork multifoil arches and diamond-pattern panels.

pp. 60-61

View of the Patio de las Doncellas by night. According to some of the many legends, this courtyard received its name in honour of the tribute of the hundred damsels.

pp. 62-63

Detail of the tilework decoration in the Patio de las Doncellas. The geometric models used in Islamic art are not mere decorative motifs but the expression of a philosophical principle revealing divine beauty.

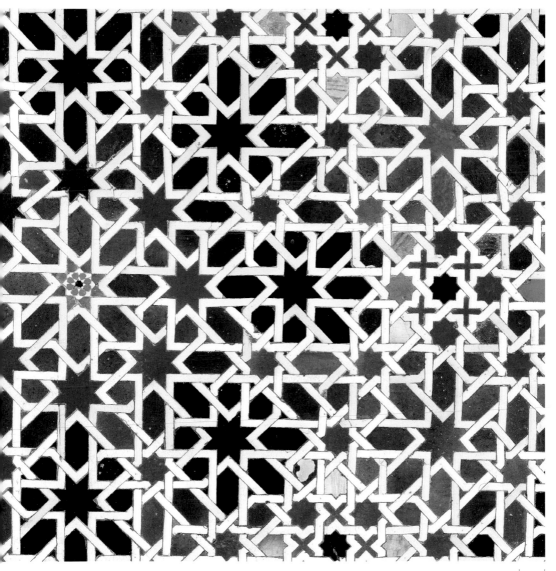

p. 64

Detail of the stuccowork in the main gallery of the Patio de las Doncellas. The gallery of multifoil arches with their surrounding *sebka* diamond-pattern decoration is one of the most distinctive artistic motifs of the Almohad dynasty.

p. 65

The Patio de las Doncellas displays two different styles: in sharp contrast with the Mudéjar main floor, the upper gallery was created to Renaissance tastes. Styles representing two completely different periods of great splendour for the Alcázar.

pp. 66-67

Detail of the ceiling in the Salón del Techo de Carlos V. A majestic example of a Renaissance ceiling consisting of coffers displaying busts of figures. This ceiling is believed to have replaced another that is now in the Mirador de los Reyes Católicos in the Cuarto Real Alto. The room itself may have been the Mudéjar Palace chapel during the reign of Peter I.

pp. 68-69

Detail of the decoration of the Salón del Techo de Carlos V. It was customary to paint the stuccowork decoration in imitation of the rich tapestries and silks used to adorn palaces.

p. 70

The ceiling in the Sala de los Infantes. Traditionally, carpentry and woodworking were assigned to master craftsmen. Many came from Toledo to work at Peter I's bidding.

p. 71

Detail of the ceiling in the Sala de los Infantes. This coffered ceiling saw the birth of the Infanta Marie Isabelle of Orléans, daughter of the Duke and Duchess of Montpensier, who for a period took up residence in the Alcázar.

p. 72

The Salón del Techo de Felipe II ("Philip II Ceiling Room"). The building was re-designed in the reign of Philip II, when new ceilings with a variety of square coffers adorned with geometric motifs were added to a number of rooms.

p. 73

The Arco de los Pavones ("Arch of the Peacocks") takes its name from the silhouettes of birds that adorn it. Outstanding are the two peacocks that frame this group of naturalistic motifs and the stylised plant motif decoration and inscriptions.

p. 74

Detail of the decoration of the door of the Salón de los Embajadores ("Hall of Ambassadors"). Built by Toledo craftsmen, the doors were decorated with ribbon motifs and, at the edges, inscriptions in Latin and Arabic. The Arabic inscription refers to the foundation of the palace and praises the king of Castile, calling him "sultan", and beseeching Allah to protect him. The Latin inscription is Psalm 54.

p. 75

View of the Patio de las Doncellas from the Salón de los Embajadores. The sheer density of the decoration makes this room the epitome of the "horror vacui" or fear of the void. The walls are veritable tapestries of colour.

p. 76

Detail of the gallery of portraits of monarchs in the Salón de los Embajadores. Above the paintings runs a band of alternating castles and lions, while above the coats of arms is a cartouche with a commemorative inscription. Painted over in the 19th century, the band was later restored.

p. 77

Detail of one of the wrought-iron balconies in the Salón de los Embajadores. These balconies were built during the reign of Philip II in the late-16th century to connect the rooms of the Cuarto Real Alto with the main areas in the Mudéjar Palace.

p. 78

Beneath a stalactite-work frame in the Salón de los Embajadores is a series of portraits of ladies by Diego de Esquivel (1599). Although anonymous, in all likelihood the ladies captured by Esquivel for posterity were courtiers.

p. 79

Each of the upper balconies in the Salón de los Embajadores is supported by three wrought-iron dragons.

p. 80

The original dome of the Salón de los Embajadores was replaced by the current one *c.* 1427 in the reign of John II. The splendour of the stars formed by ribbons on the dome is quite breathtaking. The colours, the gilding and a number of the mirrors were added in the 19th century.

p. 81

The Salón de los Embajadores may be regarded as a tribute to the two most important palaces in Al-Andalus: Medina Azahara (Cordoba) and the Alhambra (Granada), as it unites the most important architectural elements of the two historical periods. The structure of the three horseshoe arches framed by a strip of moulding known as an *alfiz* is a legacy of caliphal art, while the dome is typical of Nasrid tastes.

pp. 82-83

The Salón de los Embajadores stands at the centre of the "official" area of the Palace of Peter I. Square in shape and with a large dome, it is very similar to the Muslim *qubba*, whose square area symbolises the earth, while the dome, with its geometric decoration in the form of stars, represents the celestial sphere. It is the re-creation of a macrocosm, of the Universe.

pp. 84-85

Paintings by Diego de Esquivel (1599) in the Salón de los Embajadores. Encircling the entire room are a total of 56 portraits of Spanish monarchs —the Gothic kings and those of Leon, Castile and Spain— from Chindaswinth to Philip III. With his name above and the dates of his reign below, each king is crowned and seated and holds a sword in his right hand and a globe in the left.

ACOSTA · BITISA · EC

ONECO·A·D·7021·ONECO·A·D·7021·ONE

A ✠ EVRIGO ✠ BAMBA ✠ ROSESVNDO ✠ S

pp. 86-87

The Patio de las Muñecas lay at the centre of the private area of the Mudéjar Palace. The 14th-century main floor stands as it was originally, while the mezzanine and first floors were built in the 16th and 17th centuries and restored in the 19th century.

p. 88

Detail of the plaster decoration on the ceiling of the Patio de las Muñecas corridor. Classical ideals of beauty such as harmony and proportion are always reflected in Islamic art.

p. 89

Detail of a column, capital and arch in the Patio de las Muñecas. The base of the arch is supported by a marble capital whose entire surface is covered with plant motif decoration. The materials for these particular columns and capitals came from constructions built elsewhere and even date from other periods.

p. 90

A stucco doll's head on one of the arches of the Patio de las Muñecas. These small heads which give the courtyard its name could be the "signature" or "mark" of one of the craftsmen who worked on the area.

p. 91

Detail of one of the wooden doors in the Patio de las Muñecas. Decoration with inscriptions was a medium for propaganda in the Muslim period and a practice which continued under the kings of Castile. Words like "prosperity", "blessing", "happiness" and "grace" appear everywhere on doors and windows, together with words with religious connotations like "praise" and "glorification".

pp. 92-94
Detail of the decoration in the Salón del Techo de los Reyes Católicos. The wooden coffered ceiling combines ribbon decoration with heraldic references to the Catholic Monarchs. Represented on this shield are all the existing kingdoms on the Iberian Peninsula at the end of the 15th century; the pomegranate below suggests that the date of the ceiling is subsequent to the victory over Granada (1492). The eagle of St John stands above the shield. Also featured are the emblems of the Catholic Monarchs —the yoke, the arrows and the motto "tanto monta".

p. 95
Tileworking is a very ancient craft. Its name In Spanish (*alicatado*) is taken from that of the pliers —*allaqqat*— used to cut the ceramic pieces of which the tile is made. These pieces were fired and then assembled according to a pre-established design.

p. 96

The Cuarto del Príncipe ("Prince's Room"), so called because, according to records, Queen Isabella I of Castile gave birth to Prince John in this room in 1478. The Catholic Monarchs were overjoyed with their son and heir, but he was to die prematurely.

p. 97

Detail of the stuccowork in the Cuarto del Príncipe. Repetition and stylisation are the basic principles in the world of Islamic art, as can be seen in the calligraphic and plant motif decoration that contrasts so sharply with the Castilian heraldic motifs.

pp. 98-99

Detail of the coffered ceiling in the Cuarto del Príncipe, which dates from the 16th century. It is believed that several of the coffered ceilings were transferred from the Mudéjar rooms to the Cuarto Real Alto and that new ones were made for the main floor.

pp. 100-101

Detail of the tile decoration in the Mudéjar Palace. In Islam, symmetry, harmony, balance and order were the basic principles of artistic beauty. Geometric ornamental bow decoration made it possible to express the essence of God.

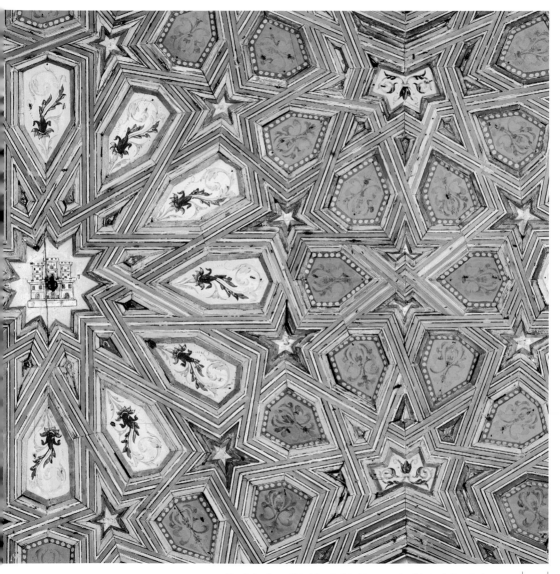

The Advent of a New Form of Art: The Gothic Palace

WITH THE ASCENSION OF ALFONSO X ("THE WISE") TO THE THRONE, THE FACE OF THE SEVILLIAN PALACE WAS TO CHANGE COMPLETELY. ALFONSO'S FATHER, THE "RECONQUEROR" OF SEVILLE, FERDINAND III ("THE SAINT"), ADAPTED THE PALACES BUILT BY THE MUSLIMS TO HIS NEEDS, FOR, FOLLOWING HIS VICTORY AT SEVILLE IN 1248, HE FREQUENTLY SPENT LONG PERIODS IN RESIDENCE AT THE ALCÁZAR, AND INDEED DIED THERE IN 1252.

FERDINAND'S SON ALFONSO WISHED TO LEAVE A CHRISTIAN MARK AND SO ORDERED MASTER CRAFTSMEN FROM BURGOS TO SEVILLE TO BUILD HIS PALACE. FRENCH INFLUENCE WAS REFLECTED IN THE RIBBED VAULTING (WHICH STILL SURVIVES) AND PILASTERS (LATER REPLACED BY THE CURRENT SUPPORTS, KNOWN AS CORBELS). IN THE MIDDLE AGES, THIS GOTHIC PALACE WAS KNOWN AS "EL CUARTO DEL CARACOL" ("THE SPIRAL APARTMENTS") BECAUSE OF THE SPIRAL STAIRCASE AT EACH OF ITS FOUR CORNERS.

BY THE TIME THIS NEW RESIDENCE HAD BEEN COMPLETED, THE OLD ALMOHAD BUILDING HAD BEEN PARTIALLY DESTROYED. BY THE REIGN OF PHILIP II, THE GOTHIC PALACE HAD FALLEN INTO SUCH A STATE OF NEGLECT THAT VARIOUS PROJECTS WERE NECESSARY TO RESTORE IT. IN 1755, THE LISBON EARTHQUAKE DESTROYED WHAT REMAINED OF THE ALMOHAD PALACE AND PART OF THE GOTHIC BUILDING, AND FURTHER PROJECTS, LED BY THE DUTCH ENGINEER SEBASTIAN VAN DER BORCHT, WERE THEN CARRIED OUT. IN THE SALA DE LOS TAPICES ("HALL OF TAPESTRIES") THE GOTHIC VAULTS (MENTIONED ABOVE) ARE ABSENT AS IT BECAME NECESSARY TO REDESIGN THIS ROOM AND ITS ENTRANCE IN THE BAROQUE PERIOD.

Detail of the tiling designed by Cristóbal de Augusta between 1577 and 1583 for the Salón de Carlos V ("Hall of Charles V").

PLVS·VLTRA

pp. 104-105

This room has been known as the Sala de las Fiestas ("Celebration Room") ever since it became the venue for the marriage of the Emperor Charles V to Isabella of Portugal. In the reign of Philip II, a number of alterations, including the addition of the windows overlooking the gardens, which bathed the room with light, were made to these rooms. The pilasters were replaced with corbels and the walls adorned with ceramics. Renaissance decoration alternates with the Emperor's coat of arms on the ceramic dado.

p. 106-107

Details of the tilework designed by Cristóbal de Augusta between 1577 and 1583 in the Sala de las Fiestas. These tiles are reminiscent of the Italian fabrics which were brought into the port of Seville by Genoese and Venetian merchants. They feature typically Renaissance elements such as cherubim, candelabra, foliage, baskets of flowers, fruit and flowers of glowing colours.

p. 108

Detail of the tiling designed by Cristóbal de Augusta between 1577 and 1583 for the Salón de Carlos V. In the 16th century, tilemakers abandoned geometric designs for other more typical themes of the age such as religious scenes, mythological characters, fabulous creatures and allegorical figures.

p. 109

Common were mythological figures in a variety of rich shades of blue, green, yellow and bright orange.

pp. 110-111

The Patio del Crucero ("Court of the Crossing") lies within the area on which the Almohad palace originally stood. It underwent alterations in the reign of Alfonso X ("The Wise") and was incorporated into the Gothic Palace. The structure was severely damaged in the Lisbon earthquake and had to be converted. The main courtyard was divided into four cross-shaped paved areas ideal for strolling in. The tops of the fruit-bearing trees and aromatic plants in the spaces between formed a canopy and created a kind of garden. Finally, a pool helped to refresh the atmosphere on hot summer's afternoons and evenings.

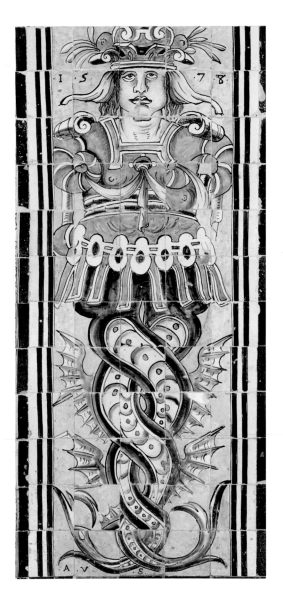

p. 112

View of the gallery leading to the Gothic Palace, with the Baños de María de Padilla ("Baths of María de Padilla") beneath the Patio del Crucero. Following excavations in recent years, the original Almohad Patio del Crucero is now clearly visible.

p. 113

The Baños de María de Padilla. All the spaces in this area are situated in the cellars of the Patio del Crucero. Built during the period of the Almohad dynasty in the 12th century, the baths were transformed by Alfonso X, who added the ribbed vaulting. In the Renaissance period, a fountain which emptied into the pool was also added.

pp. 114-115

The Salón de los Tapices ("Hall of Tapestries") and the Salones de Carlos V ("Halls of Charles V"). Due to the damage caused by the Lisbon earthquake, in 1755 a series of projects affecting the original layout and conception of the whole complex was carried out. Two results of the reconstruction work were the Salón de los Tapices and the Patio del Crucero gateway.

pp. 116-117

The Map, chronologically the first tapestry in the *Conquest of Tunis* series. It features a map of Tunisia and the Mediterranean area as seen from Europe.

p. 118

The Capture of Tunis, one of the six tapestries exhibited in the Salón de los Tapices in the Gothic Palace. This series of tapestries relating the conquest of Tunis by Charles V in 1535 were commissioned by the Emperor himself in 1554. They were woven at the Pannemaker workshop in Brussels from cartoons painted by Jan Cornelisz Vermeyen. Pannemaker's factory was one of the most prestigious of the age and its tapestries were always in great demand. The exhibits now on display are copies ordered by Philip V from the Royal Tapestry Factory in Madrid in 1740 due to the deterioration of the originals.

p. 119

The chapel in the Gothic palace was restored in the 16th century along the same lines as the other rooms. It is dominated by a copy of the *Our Lady of La Antigua* in Seville Cathedral.

MAR ATHLANTICO.

MAR DE BERVERIA.

MAR DE NVMIDIA

Estre cho de gibraltar.

MARDESPANA

MAR OCCIDENTAL

Cuenta de leguas.
Cuenta de millas.

ERE CAESAR   COMPARAT HINC CLASSES. ET. SIGNA MINANTIA POENIS
SSA SEQVENTEM. SIGNIS. HESPERIASQ. RATES. LIGVRVMQ CARINAS.
BELLA MOVETEM SICQ. MORAE IMPATIENS DVM TEMPVS ET HORA FEREBAT.

ADMOVET INFESTVS CAROLVS IAM SIGNA THVNETO
ATQVE SVBVRBANVS CAPITVR DVM VICVS AB ARCE
SIGNIFICAT CAPTIVA MANVS QVAE ERGASTVLA MVRO
SVEFOSSO ET FORIBVS FRACTIS CRISTOQVE SECVNDO

LIQVIT ET EXCLVSO TENET HANC CVSTODE EIDEMQVE
VINDICIS IMPLORAT CAROLI: CHARADINVS AB VRBE
AVFVGIT IRRVMPIT CAESAR CAPTAMQVE PER VRBEM
PERGIT ET OPTATAM GRADITVR AVGVSTVS AD ARCEM.

A Secluded Paradise:
The Alcázar Gardens

LIKE THE PALACE, THE GARDENS HAVE UNDERGONE MANY CHANGES OVER THE AGES.

ALL THE PALACES OF AL ANDALUS HAD GARDEN-ORCHARDS WITH FRUIT TREES, HORTICULTURAL PRODUCE AND A WIDE VARIETY OF FRAGRANT FLOWERS. WATER, THAT GREAT MIRACLE OF ISLAM, WAS EVER-PRESENT IN MUSLIM GARDENS IN THE FORM OF FOUNTAINS, RUNNELS, JETS, PONDS, IRRIGATION CHANNELS AND POOLS. THE GARDEN-ORCHARDS NOT ONLY SUPPLIED FOOD FOR THE PALACE RESIDENTS BUT ALSO FULFILLED AN AESTHETIC FUNCTION BY BRINGING PLEASURE TO ALL FIVE SENSES. IT MIGHT BE SAID THAT THESE EXTRAORDINARY PLACES WERE ATTEMPTS TO RE-CREATE HEAVEN ON EARTH.

THE HISPANO-MUSLIM GARDENS ADJOINING THE WALLS OF THE PALACIO DE DON PEDRO I AND THE GOTHIC PALACE WERE REDESIGNED IN THE 16TH CENTURY DURING THE REIGNS OF THE EMPEROR CHARLES V AND PHILIP II. THE REIGN OF PHILIP III SAW THE ARRIVAL OF ONE OF THE GREAT ITALIAN ARTISTS OF THE AGE, VERMONDO RESTA, WHO LEFT HIS HALLMARK ON THE GARDENS IN THE FORM OF THE ITALIAN MANNERIST STYLE THAT WAS SO IN VOGUE IN THE EARLY-17TH CENTURY.

SPAIN'S ARABIAN GARDENS BECAME ALL THE RAGE IN THE 19TH CENTURY, THANKS TO THE EUROPEAN ROMANTIC TRAVELLERS, WHO PRAISED THEIR EXOTIC, DREAM-LIKE, EASTERN QUALITIES. ALSO APPARENT IS THE NATURALISTIC REINTERPRETATION OF ENGLISH LANDSCAPE GARDENING AND, IN THE EARLY DECADES OF THE 20TH CENTURY, A REGIONALIST APPROACH TO GARDENS.

Statue of the god *Mercury* (1575), designed by Diego de Pesquera and cast by Bartolomé Morel (creator of the *Giraldillo* statue, which crowns the Giralda tower in Seville) on the Estanque de Mercurio ("Pond of Mercury").

p. 122

The Galería de Grutesco ("Grotto Gallery"). Between 1612 and 1621 the Italian artist Vermondo Resta transformed the old Muslim wall into a loggia of fanciful forms from which to admire the view of the palace gardens.

p. 123

The Mannerist-style decoration in the Galería de los Grutescos is a fusion of architecture and nature, with rocks appearing to emerge from out of the building. The stones resemble sea rocks and were brought from various sources.

pp. 124-125

The Estanque de Mercurio was originally an irrigation reservoir whose water came from a Roman aqueduct which was adapted by the Muslims and is known today as the Caños de Carmona. The aqueduct brought the water from the River Guadaira to the Alcázar across the wall separating the palace and the old Jewish quarter.

p. 126

The rocks rising in the gallery imitate the natural appearance of caves in a technique known in Spanish as "labor de grutesco" ("grotto work"). The word *grutesco* comes from the Italian *grotta* meaning grotto.

p. 127

The Roman god Mercury (Hermes in Greek mythology) is regarded as both the messenger of the gods and the god of commerce. His name is related to the Latin word *merx* (merchandise). The patron of highways and a guide to travellers, he is usually depicted wearing a helmet and winged sandals and holding a staff with two intertwined snakes coiled around it.

p. 128

The Jardín del Chorrón takes its name from the water that runs into the Estanque de Mercurio. An area of the court wall is covered with wisteria, a climbing plants with purple flowers. Adjoining it is the old Jardín de la Alcubilla ("Reservoir Garden"), also known as the Patio del Tenis ("Tennis yard"), as it once boasted the first tennis court ever built in Spain (early-20th century).

p. 129

The wall of the gallery overlooking the Estanque de Mercurio is adorned with frescoes. The red tones imitate red marble. The mythological figures and exotic birds were painted by Diego de Esquivel.

pp. 130-131

The Jardín de las Flores ("Garden of the Flowers"). The Hornacina de Carlos V ("Charles V Niche"), by Vermondo Resta, late-16th to early-17th century. The structure is adorned with typically Mannerist-style seashells.

p.132

The Jardín de las Flores. The pool is decorated with tiles by Pisano (late-16th to early-17th century). Typical of this kind of courtyard, the orange trees on trellises along the walls create a pleasant atmosphere with cool, shady areas in summer.

p. 133

The Jardín de las Damas ("Garden of the Ladies") was redesigned during the 16th and 17th centuries. The fountains and Mannerist portals were designed by Vermondo Resta. Of interest are the water spouts in the ground which could be triggered from one of the benches to provide amusement for guests or to catch them unawares and splash them.

pp. 134-135

The pond in the Jardín de las Flores (detail of Pisano's tiling). The Muslim influence in these small gardens is evident in a clear example of the division of the Patio —as in the case of the Patio del Crucero— into four parts. Each area contains trees and an abundance of plants with fragrant, bright and colourful flowers.

pp. 136-137

One of the fountains in the Jardín de las Damas is known as the Fuente de la Fama ("Fountain of Fame"). Dating from the 17th century, it was designed by the Italian architect Vermondo Resta. Fountains of this type were first made in Italy in the late-16th century. This one uses the power of water and wind to play pieces of 17th-century popular and religious music.

p. 138

A statue of Neptune, god of the sea, atop the fountain at the centre of the Jardín de las Damas.

p. 139

The Fuente del Monte Parnaso ("Fountain of Mount Parnassus") in the Jardín del Laberinto ("Maze Garden") or Jardín de la Cruz ("Garden of the Cross"). The fountain is the last vestige of the old 16th- century Jardín del Laberinto, which ceased to exist in 1910. This rendering of Mount Parnassus was adorned with mythological allegories containing embedded waterspouts. Though little of it remains today, it is thought to have depicted the god Apollo surrounded by the nine Muses.

pp.140-141

The Jardín del Laberinto. This modern
maze was designed in 1914. Of myrtle,
cypress and white cedar, it was Renais-
sance-inspired.

pp. 142-143

The Jardín del Cenador de la Alcoba ("Garden of the Bedroom Pavilion"). This pavilion was built especially for the marriage of the Emperor Charles V and Isabella of Portugal. Originally a Muslim building, it is a mixture of traditional Mudéjar and Renaissance styles. It is also a clear example of how over the ages the former managed to survive and even coexist with other styles from elsewhere in Europe. This square pavilion with its magnificent coffered ceiling and fountain at the centre is decorated with press-mould technique tiles. Windows in each of the four sides allow a cool breeze to enter the pavilion on summer nights.

pp. 144-145

The tiling in the Pabellón de Carlos V ("Pavilion of Charles V") was made in the 16th century at the Polido brothers workshop with the press-mould technique and adorned with motifs known as "grotesques" that combine leaf decoration with fabulous creatures. The press-mould technique consists of pressing a decorated negative mould onto fresh clay to leave a design with reliefs that will prevent colours from mixing when they are applied.

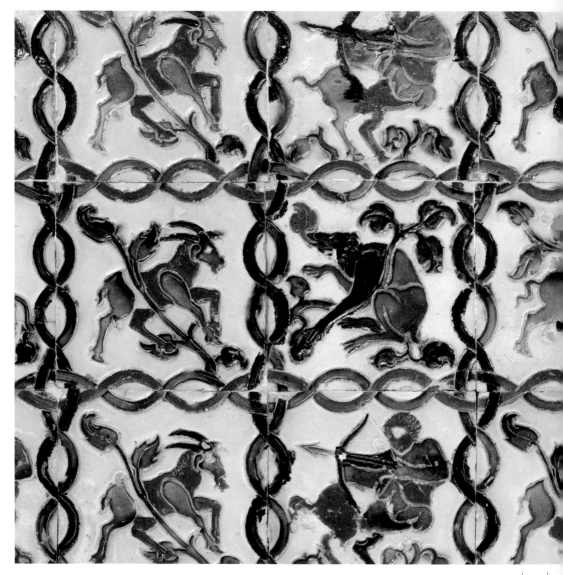

p. 146

The Jardín de los Poetas ("Garden of the Poets") lies on the site of the old Huerta del Retiro ("Garden of Retreat") on the other side of the Galería de los Grutescos. Designed in 1956, its two large ponds flank a fountain.

p. 147

The Cenador del León ("Lion Pavilion"), dominated by a statue of a lion. This pavilion and fountain were designed in the 17th century.

p. 148

A floor decorated with tiles in the Jardín del Marqués de la Vega-Inclán ("Marquis of La Vega-Inclán Garden"). Dating from the late-19th century, this garden is a beautiful area full of fountains, channels and waterspouts with benches, runnels and flooring adorned with ceramics. In the picture, a detail of the typically Andalusian fired clay and tiled floor.

p. 149

The famous 15th-century Puerta de Marchena ("Marchena Gateway") originally from the family home of the Dukes of Arcos. It was transferred from the palace in Arcos, Seville, to the Alcázar in 1913.

When we gathered early in the morning to bid farewell,
banners were already fluttering in the courtyard of the Alcázar,
steeds were brought forward and kettledrums rolled:
these were the signals for our leaving. [...]

Departure, *Al Mutamid*

Biographical notes

MUHAMMAD IBN 'ABBAD AL-MU'TAMID
Beja (Portugal), 1040 - Agmat, (Morocco), 1095.

Born into the Abbadid family, who ruled Seville in the 11th century, he was the second son and successor of al-Mutadid (1042-1069). King of the *taifa* kingdom of Seville from 1069 to 1090, after which he was exiled to Africa, where he died some years later. A renowned poet, Al-Mu'tamid fostered an exceptional cultural environment in Seville. Traditionally his palace, the *Al-Qasr al-Mubarak* ("Fortress of the Blessing"), is believed to have been situated on the current site of the Palacio de Don Pedro I ("Palace of Peter I").

ABU YA'QUB YUSUF
Marrakech (Morocco), 1135 - Santarém (Portugal), 1184.

King of the Almohad dynasty from 1163. He settled in Seville in 1171, making it the capital of his empire. A great patron of culture, he was one of the most cultivated and popular monarchs of his time. It was he who built the *alcazaba* or citadel (today the site of the Alcázar) and the mosque with its minaret (now the Cathedral and the tower known as the "Giralda"). He died at the Battle of Santarém fighting Ferdinand II of Leon in 1184.

FERDINAND III OF CASTILE AND LEON
Zamora or Ciudad Real (?), 1199 - Seville, 1252

Son of Alfonso IX, King of Leon, and Berenguela I, Queen of Castile. During his reign he united the crowns of Castile and Leon. He recovered Cordoba (1236), Murcia (1243), Jaen (1245) and Seville (1248), occupying the palaces abandoned by the Muslims during his long periods of residence in those cities. Canonised in 1671, he is buried in the Royal Chapel in Seville Cathedral.

ALFONSO X OF CASTILE AND LEON
Toledo, 1221 - Seville, 1284

Son of Ferdinand III and Beatrice of Swabia. As heir to the throne of Castile and Leon, he extended his father's policy of reconquest, occupying cities such as Jerez (1253) and Cadiz (1262). As the son of Beatrice of Swabia, he aspired to the throne of the Holy Roman Empire, but, despite devoting a considerable part of his life to this cause, was unsuccessful. It was Alfonso X ("The Wise") who built the Gothic Palace —one of most important political and cultural centres in mediaeval Europe— at the Alcázar in Seville.

ALFONSO XI OF CASTILE AND LEON
Salamanca, 1311 - Gibraltar, 1350

With Alfonso XI's victory at the Battle of Río Salado in 1340 and conquest of the kingdom of Algeciras in 1344, the limits of the Christian kingdom finally stretched as far as the Straits of Gibraltar. It was during his reign that the Sala de la Justicia ("Hall of Justice") was built at the Alcázar in Seville. On the annulment of his first marriage, he married Mary of Portugal, who provided an heir to the crown of Castile, Peter I. However, in an extramarital liaison with Leonor de Guzmán, Alfonso sired ten other children, one of whom, Don Enrique, was to murder his stepbrother, King Peter, in Montiel in 1369 and ascend the throne as Henry II.

PETER I OF CASTILE
Burgos, 1334 - Montiel, 1369

The last King of Castile of the House of Burgundy, after whose assassination the crown passed to the House of Trastámara.

Peter is historically known as "the Cruel" (as he was dubbed by his enemies), but centuries later Philip II, who believed that the chronicles of Peter's age had been unfair, nicknamed him "The Just". With the construction of the Mudéjar Palace during Peter's reign, the Alcázar at Seville saw its age of greatest splendour.

ISABELLA I OF CASTILE AND LEON
Madrigal de las Altas Torres (Avila), 1451 - Medina del Campo (Valladolid) 1504
The daughter of John II of Castile and Isabella of Portugal, Isabella inherited the kingdom of Castile on the death of her step-brother Henry IV in 1474. She married Ferdinand II of Aragon in the Palace of the Viveros, Valladolid, in 1469. Both she and her husband spent long periods in Seville. During their first stay in 1477, they ordered sections of the Cuarto Real Alto ("Upper Royal Apartments") built. Isabella gave birth to her only son, Prince John, in the Alcázar's Mudéjar Palace.

FERDINAND II OF ARAGON
Sos del Rey Católico (Aragon), 1452 - Madrigalejo (Caceres), 1516
Ferdinand was proclaimed King of Sicily in 1468 and King of Aragon on the death of his father, John II, in 1479. When Isabella died in 1504, their daughter Joan was proclaimed Queen of Castile. In 1505, the king married Germaine de Foix. The name "Catholic Monarchs" comes from a papal bull, the second bull *Inter Caetera* of 1493, which was drafted after the complete re-

conquest of the Iberian Peninsula from the Muslims and the monarchs' stated intention to evangelise the New World. It described the monarchs as "Catholicos reges, et principes".

CHARLES I
Ghent, 1500 - Monastery of Yuste (Caceres), 1558
Charles was to rule one of the greatest empires of the modern era. He was the son of Joan I of Castile and Philip I of Habsburg and grandson of Maximilian I of Austria and Mary of Burgundy, from whom he inherited the Netherlands, the Austrian territories and the birthright to the imperial throne. From his mother he inherited Castile, Naples, Sicily, the Indies, Aragon and the Canary Islands. As King of Spain he ruled as Charles I and as Emperor of the Holy Roman Empire as Charles V. The Emperor's name is closely linked to the history of the Alcázar at Seville as he chose it for his marriage to Isabella of Portugal in 1526.

PHILIP II
Valladolid, 1527 - San Lorenzo de El Escorial (Madrid), 1598
The son and heir of Charles I of Spain and Isabella of Portugal, Philip was King of Spain from 1556 until his death in 1598. He ruled a vast empire formed by Castile, Aragon, Catalonia, Navarre, Valencia, the Roussillon, the Franche-Comté, the Netherlands, Sicily, Sardinia, Milan, Naples, Oran, Tunisia, Portugal and its imperial territories in Africa and Asia, Spanish America and the Philippines. Seville saw its heyday during Philip's reign when it became the centre for the Indies trade monopoly and a cosmopolitan city with one of the largest populations of the

age. Philip II visited Seville for 15 days in 1570. He took up residence in the Alcázar and ordered major alterations made.

PHILIP III
Madrid, 1578 - Madrid, 1621

The reign of Philip II's son marked the beginning of the decline of the Spanish Empire. From the outset, the king delegated affairs of state to favourites, the best-known being the Duke of Lerma. It was during his reign (1609) that the expulsion of the Moriscos was decreed. For Philip's visit to Seville, one of the finest architects of the first half of the 17th century, the Milanese Vermondo Resta (who left a Mannerist hallmark on the Alcázar, particularly the gardens), was commissioned. Philip's visit to the city, however, was cut short by his sudden death.

PHILIP IV
Valladolid, 1605 - Madrid, 1665

Philip IV ascended the throne following his father's sudden death in 1621. A generous patron of culture, he promoted literature, the arts and theatre. It was during his reign that Spain saw its Golden Age, a cultural climax in sharp contrast with the economic and social crises of the age. Philip delegated affairs of state to his favourites, particularly the Count-Duke of Olivares, who arranged a thirteen-day visit by the king to Seville. The alterations to the Alcázar begun by Philip III continued until Philip IV's stay, but thereafter the building underwent a period of neglect and decline.

PHILIP V
Versailles, 1683 - Madrid, 1746

The French prince Philip of Bourbon became King of Spain and first monarch of the Bourbon dynasty in November 1700. He succeeded through his great-uncle Charles II, the last King of Spain of the Habsburg dynasty. His reign, which can be divided into two main periods, is regarded as the longest of any Spanish monarch, lasting 45 years and 3 days. During the first part of his reign, Philip, his second wife Isabella Farnese and their family took up residence in Seville. This period is known as the "Royal Lustrum", as the royal sojourn lasted five years, from 1729 until 1733. It was during this period that the Alcázar of Seville regained its splendour.

CHARLES III
Madrid, 1716 - Madrid, 1788

Charles III was proclaimed Duke of Parma in 1731 and King of Naples and Sicily in 1734. He was King of Spain from 1759 until his death in 1788. He succeeded his brothers Louis, who reigned for a short time as Louis I, and Ferdinand VI. As a child, Charles lived with his family in Seville for five years. During his reign Pablo de Olavide was appointed Chief Officer of Justice of Seville, becoming highly influential in the city's affairs. Important meetings and gatherings attended by the most scholarly figures of the age were held in the Alcázar. After much of the Alcázar was destroyed in the Lisbon earthquake of 1755, it was subsequently rebuilt.

Detail of the tilework decoration in the Mudéjar Palace.

CHARLES IV
Portici, Naples, 1748 - Rome 1819

Charles IV succeeded his father Charles III in 1788. During his reign the Spanish economy deteriorated progressively. The first years were marked by the policies of the ministers Floridablanca and the Count of Aranda, and from 1793 the country was controlled by the king's *valido* or favourite, Manuel Godoy. Deposed by his son Ferdinand VII in 1808 after the Mutiny of Aranjuez, he died in exile in Italy. During Charles IV's reign, a Spanish royal family again visited the Alcázar of Seville, taking up residence there for eleven days in 1796.

ISABELLA II
Madrid, 1830 - Paris, 1904

Isabella was proclaimed heiress to the Spanish throne on the death of her father Ferdinand VII when she only three years of age. The abolition of the Salic Law of Succession in her favour led the country into a prolonged conflict with Carlos Maria Isidro de Bourbon, Ferdinand VII's brother, who claimed his right of succession. She spent several periods in the Alcázar of Seville, where she ordered far-reaching alterations and a programme of pictorial restoration affecting virtually the whole of the palace.

ALFONSO XII
Madrid, 1857 - El Pardo (Madrid), 1885

King of Spain from 1874 to 1885, his premature death from tuberculosis at 27 years of age left his son, Alfonso XIII, whom he never saw, heir to the throne. His second wife, Maria Cristina of Austria, was regent of Spain until her son came of age in 1902. Alfonso XII married twice: his first wife, his cousin Mercedes, daughter of the duc de Montpensier, died only a few months after their wedding in 1878. The setting for their love story can be said to have been Seville, as Alfonso XII resided at the Real Alcázar for long periods and Mercedes lived at the Palacio de San Telmo, also in the city.

ALFONSO XIII
Madrid, 1886 - Rome, 1941

The posthumous son of Alfonso XII, Alfonso XIII was King of Spain from birth until the proclamation of the Second Republic on 14th April, 1931, when the Spanish royal family went into exile in France and later Italy. Alfonso XIII and his wife visited Seville several times and the king himself took charge of the work for the Ibero-American Exposition of 1929. During this period various refurbishment programmes were carried out at the Alcázar by the Marquis of la Vega Inclán. On 22nd April, 1931, the government of the Second Spanish Republic ceded the Alcázar and its gardens to the Seville City Council.

JUAN CARLOS I
Rome, 1938

The current Head of the Spanish Royal Household. As a child he lived in Lausanne (Switzerland) and Estoril (Portugal). He came to Spain for the first time in 1948, at 10 years of age, when his father and General Francisco Franco agreed that he should be educated in Spain. He was crowned king on 22nd November, 1975, shortly after Franco's death. On 12th April, 1988, the Seville City Council authorised the use of the area of the Alcázar known as the Cuarto Real Alto ("Upper Royal Quarters") as an official residence of the Spanish royal family. The Alcázar of Seville was witness to the celebration of the marriage of Juan Carlos's daughter, the Infanta Elena, to Jaime de Marichalar in 1995, when the couple also became the Duke and Duchess of Lugo.

Detail of the tilework decoration of the Arco de los Pavones, Mudéjar Palace.

Map

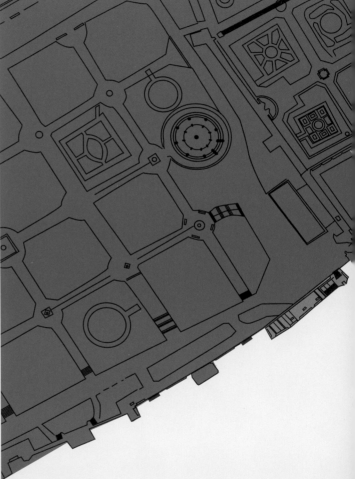

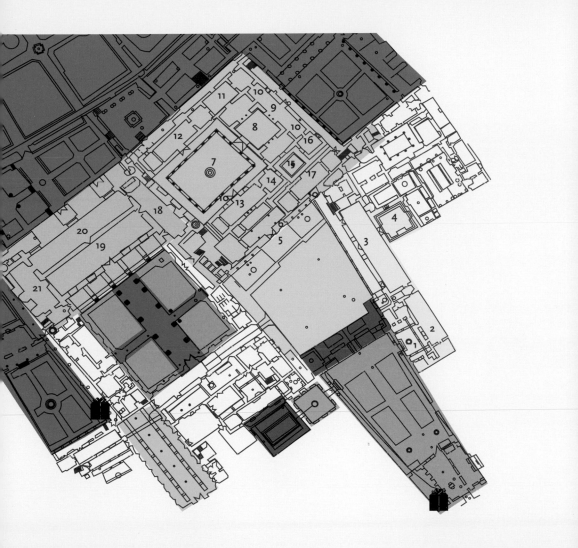

Gardens

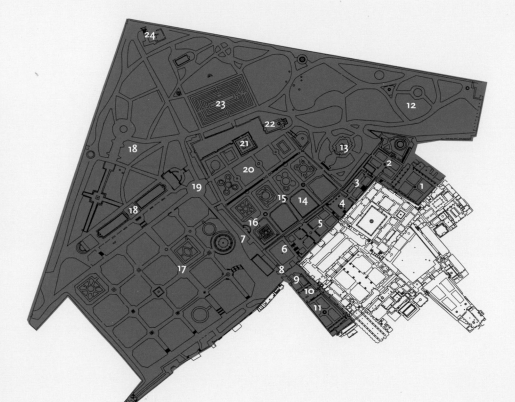

1. Prince's Garden
2. Garden of the Flowers
3. Garden of the Galley
4. Garden of Troy
5. Garden of Dance
6. Pond of Mercury
7. Grotto Gallery
8. Marchena Gateway
9. Garden of the Stream
10. Chinesischer Pavillon
11. Reservoir Garden
12. English Garden
13. Garden of the Maze
14. Garden of the Ladies
15. Fountain of Neptune
16. Fountain of Fame
17. La Vega-Inclán Garden
18. Garden of the Poets
19. Privilege Gate
20. Bedroom Garden
21. Pavilion of Charles V
22. Lion Pavilion
23. New Maze Garden
24. Almohadischer Turm